W9-DHH-853

Library of Congress Cataloging-in-Publication Data

Watts, Barrie.
    Dandelion.

    (Stopwatch books)
    Includes index.
    Summary: Describes in simple text and illustrations
how a dandelion changes from a flower to a dandelion
clock and how the seeds are blown away.
    1. Dandelions — Juvenile literature. 2. Dandelions —
Reproduction — Juvenile literature. [1. Dandelions]
I. Title. II. Series.
QK495.C74W34   1987   583 .55   86-31501
ISBN 0-382-09442-5
ISBN 0-382-09438-7 (lib. bdg.)

First published by A & C Black (Publishers) Limited
35 Bedford Row, London WC1R 4JH

© 1987 Barrie Watts

Published in the United States in 1987
by Silver Burdett Press,
Englewood Cliffs, New Jersey

Acknowledgements
The artwork is by Helen Senior
The publishers would like to thank Jean Imrie and Simon Ryder for their help and
advice.

Dandelion

Barrie Watts

Stopwatch books

Silver Burdett Press • Englewood Cliffs, New Jersey

Here is a dandelion.

Have you ever seen these flowers?
They are dandelions. You can find them in gardens and by roadsides.

Most plants can flower only in spring and summer, but dandelions can have flowers almost all year round. There are lots of different kinds of dandelions. All of them have leaves with jagged edges.

This book will tell you how dandelions make their seeds.

The dandelion flowers open.

On sunny days, the dandelion flowers open. Each flower is at the end of a long stalk. If you pick a dandelion, you can see that the stalk is hollow like a straw.

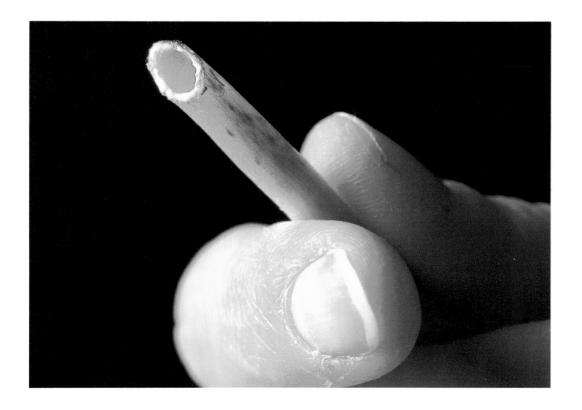

Have you ever noticed the sticky white juice that comes out of the stalk? It is food for the plant. If you get this juice on your skin or your clothes it leaves brown marks.

Insects visit the flower.

A dandelion flower is made up of lots of tiny flowers growing very close together. This dandelion has been cut in half.

Each tiny flower is joined to the main stalk. The tiny flowers are smaller near the middle of the dandelion.

Inside each tiny flower there is some sweet juice called nectar. Wasps and other insects visit the dandelion because they eat the nectar.

The dandelion grows seeds.

The dandelion flower only stays open for a few days.
Then it closes and the petals start to dry up and die.
This drawing shows the closed flower cut in half.

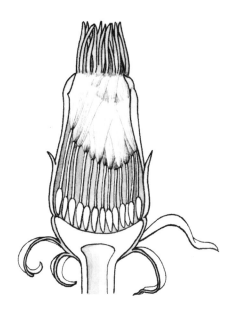

Tiny seeds are beginning to grow underneath the dried
up petals. They are soft and green. Each one has a tiny
stalk growing from it, with soft white hairs at the top.

Look at the big photograph. A week later you can see the
white tips just showing. The green sepals around the
flower keep the seeds safe until they are ripe.

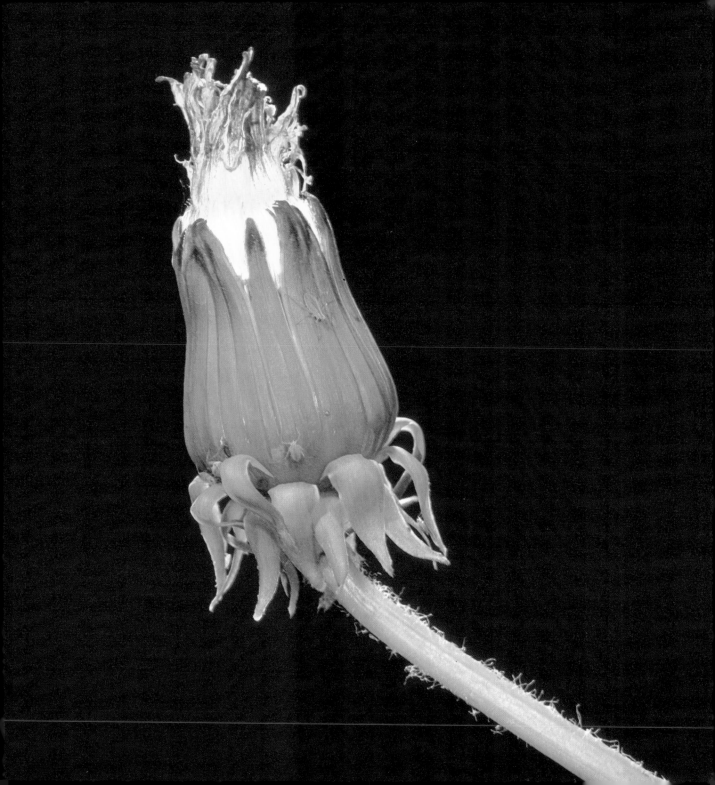

The dandelion head opens again.

When the seeds are fully grown, the dead petals drop off and the dandelion head opens again. Look at the big photograph. This dandelion is opening.

The white hairs attached to the seeds are still damp and closed. You can't see the seeds yet. They are hidden inside.

After fifteen minutes, the seed head is half open.

Now you can see the seeds. They have turned brown. The green sepals are folding back. Soon they will dry up and die.

The seed parachutes open.

The dandelion head has fully opened. It is as big as a golf ball. The outside is soft and fluffy. The white hairs have dried and opened into tiny parachutes.
Each parachute is attached to one seed.

The balls made of parachutes and seeds are sometimes called dandelion clocks. Look at the small photograph.

How many dandelion clocks can you see?

The seeds make a pattern.

Each seed and its parachute is very small. Here is one next to a pin.

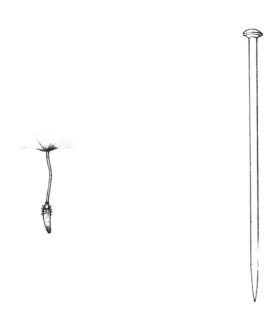

Now look at the photograph. Some seeds have been taken out of this dandelion clock.

The top of the stalk looks like a pin cushion. It has lots of tiny dents to hold the seeds. A dandelion clock can have as many as 180 seeds. All the seeds are the same size and they always match together to make the same pattern.

The dandelion seeds blow away.

When the seeds are ripe, they are only loosely attached to the stalk. The wind lifts the parachutes up into the air and the seeds are blown away.

Soon all the seeds have gone and the stalk is bare.

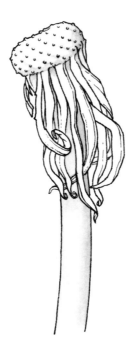

It will dry up and die. Next year the dandelion will grow more leaves and flowers.

The seed is carried a long way from the plant.

The seed is hard and has tiny hooks on it. It is very light.
The seed is blown along by the wind. It can be carried
a long way from the plant. If the seed lands on some soil,
it may start to grow.

Sometimes a seed lands on an animal, and the tiny hooks
hold it in the animal's hair. If the animal scratches or
brushes the seed away, it may fall on some soil and
start to grow.

A tiny plant starts to grow.

Look at the big photograph. This seed has started to grow. It has grown roots and leaves. Can you see the parachute sticking up out of the soil next to the plant?

After a few days the plant is bigger. It has grown more leaves. It needs water, light, and air to live and grow.

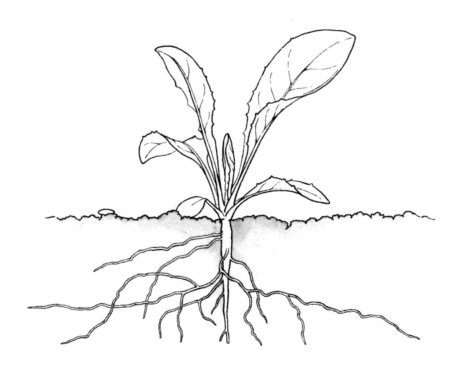

The plant takes in water through its roots. Its leaves spread out to get light and air.

The dandelion plant grows buds.

A year later, the dandelion plant is much bigger. Some flower buds have appeared on the plant. They are still tightly closed.

On a sunny day, they will start to open. Look at the big photograph. The petals are just beginning to show.

What do you think will happen to the dandelion flower?

Do you remember how a dandelion plant makes its seeds?
See if you can tell the story in your own words.
You can use these pictures to help you.

3

6

Index

This will help you to
find some of the important
words in the book.

See if you can find a dandelion clock. What does it feel like?
Blow it and watch where the seeds land. What does the stalk look like?